EXPLORE OUR WORLD

LIFE SCIENCE

Curious Cats

MICHÈLE DUFRESNE

TABLE OF CONTENTS

Are Cats Curious?... 2
Why Do Cats Like Boxes?................................. 6
Why Do Cats Have Whiskers? 10
Do Cats Hate Water?.. 14
Do Cats Really Have Nine Lives?................... 19
Glossary/Index.. 20

PIONEER VALLEY EDUCATIONAL PRESS, INC

ARE CATS CURIOUS?

There is an old saying that curiosity killed the cat. But what does that mean?

It is true that cats are curious **creatures**. Being curious teaches them about the world around them. As **predators**, they must be able to explore their surroundings.

A cat's home is its **territory**. Cats are very curious about their territory, and they want to know everything about it. They will often inspect their territory for possible threats and places to hide.

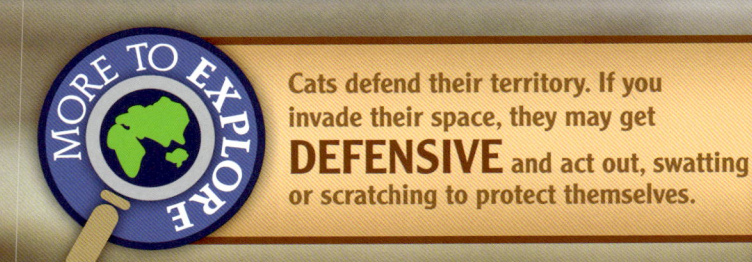

MORE TO EXPLORE

Cats defend their territory. If you invade their space, they may get **DEFENSIVE** and act out, swatting or scratching to protect themselves.

Sometimes there is a place in a cat's territory that it cannot explore, like a locked closet or a closed trunk. This can make a cat very anxious. It may wonder if something dangerous lives in the closet.

Or could there be something interesting inside the trunk? Cats like to know everything about their territory.

WHY DO CATS LIKE BOXES?

Have you ever noticed that cats love to go inside boxes? One reason for this may be that boxes provide a place for cats to hide. Cats are predators. A cat can hide in a box and not be seen while it quietly waits for its **prey** to walk by.

Boxes also provide a safe place to take a nap. Cats can sleep for 18-20 hours every day. They may feel safer sleeping inside a box. They may feel like they are hidden away from anything dangerous. Cats that live in the wild do not have boxes to sleep in. Instead, they will hide in treetops, dens, and caves.

A group of **researchers** studied homeless cats
that were brought to an animal shelter.
Some of the cats were given a box,
and some were not. The researchers found
that the cats with a box were calmer
and happier than the cats without a box.
The cats with a box had an easier time getting
used to their new home at the shelter.
They were also friendlier with **humans**.

Cats also like boxes because the small space inside a box can help keep them warm.

MORE TO EXPLORE

Cats like to get in other **SMALL SPACES**, like a bathroom sink, shoes, and even shopping bags.

WHY DO CATS HAVE WHISKERS?

Many people know that cats have whiskers under their noses. But cats also have whiskers on other parts of their bodies.
Long, stiff hairs grow above their eyes, on their chins, and near their feet.

Whiskers on a cat can shed, but you should never trim them.

Some people think that cats' whiskers
are like human hairs, but this is not true.
Cats' whiskers are connected to **nerves**.
When cats brush against something,
their whiskers tell them things about the object.
Their whiskers can tell them where the object
is and how large it is.

Whiskers can also allow cats to move around
in the dark or find a hole to hide in.
This can help cats stay safe from predators.

You can look at a cat's whiskers and learn something about how that cat is feeling. If a cat's whiskers are pulled back across its face, then the cat may feel threatened by something. When a cat's whiskers are pointed away from its face, then the cat is feeling relaxed.

MORE TO EXPLORE

Many mammals have **WHISKERS**. Scientists think that mammals have whiskers to help them find food and make their way around in the dark.

13

DO CATS HATE WATER?

Many people believe that cats hate water, but some cats enjoy getting wet.

Some wild cats live in hot, dry places and will jump in the water to cool down and to catch fish to eat.

Cats that live in very cold places will stay away from water. They know it is hard to stay warm when they are wet.

MORE TO EXPLORE

The Asian fishing cat is an excellent swimmer. It has **WEBBED PAWS** that help it to catch prey in the water.

Many house cats are very interested in water. They will dip their paws into a bowl of water. They will also run into the bathroom when they hear the sound of water running in the sink or shower.

>> A dripping faucet can look like a fun toy to a cat. A cat will try to catch drops of water as the faucet drips.

Cats do not often need a bath. They are clean animals. They use their tongues to clean themselves. But if a cat gets into something sticky or smelly, it may need a bath. Cats that are bathed often when they are young grow used to being in the water.

To give a cat a bath, start by placing it in an empty tub or sink and talking to it softly. Then run a washcloth with warm water over its fur. If the cat is calm, you can fill the bath with warm water. Make sure the water is not too hot or cold. Then use a pitcher to slowly pour water over the cat's fur. After the bath, dry your cat off with a fluffy towel and tell it how brave it was.

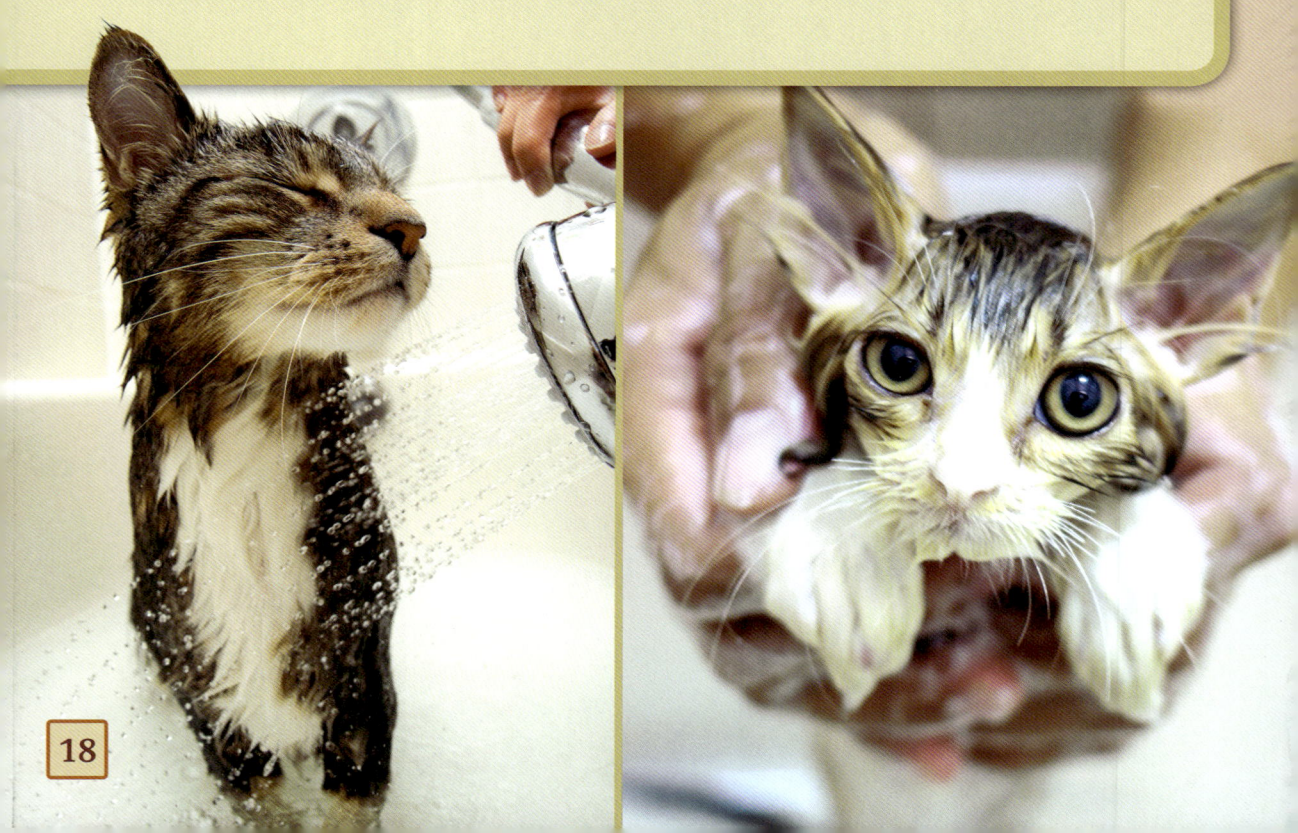